ideals CHRISTMAS

50 Years of Celebrating Life's Most Treasured Moments

Vol. 51, No. 8

"Christmas is a quest. May each of us follow his star of faith and find the heart's own Bethlehem."

—Esther Baldwin York

Country Chronicle
9

50 Years Ago
52

For the Children
12

Legendary Americans
56

A Slice of Life
16

Bits & Pieces
60

Readers' Reflections
20

Ideals' Family Recipes
66

Traveler's Diary
24

From My Garden Journal
70

Collector's Corner
42

Handmade Heirloom
72

Through My Window
46

Readers' Forum
78

IDEALS—Vol. 51, No. 8 December MCMXCIV IDEALS (ISSN 0019-137X) is published eight times a year: February, March, May, June, August, September, November, December by IDEALS PUBLICATIONS INCORPORATED, 565 Marriott Drive, Suite 800, Nashville, TN 37214. Second-class postage paid at Nashville, Tennessee, and additional mailing offices. Copyright © MCMXCIV by IDEALS PUBLICATIONS INCORPORATED. POSTMASTER: Send address changes to Ideals, PO Box 148000, Nashville, TN 37214-8000. All rights reserved. Title IDEALS registered U.S. Patent Office.

SINGLE ISSUE—$4.95
ONE-YEAR SUBSCRIPTION—eight consecutive issues as published—$19.95
TWO-YEAR SUBSCRIPTION—sixteen consecutive issues as published—$35.95
Outside U.S.A., add $6.00 per subscription year for postage and handling.

Printed and bound in USA by The Banta Company, Menasha, Wisconsin.

Printed on Weyerhaeuser Husky.

The paper used in this publication meets the minimum requirements of American National Standard for Information Sciences— Permanence of Paper for Printed Library Materials, ANSI Z39.48-1984.

Unsolicited manuscripts will not be returned without a self-addressed, stamped envelope.

ISBN 0-8249-1122-9

Cover Photo, RINGING IN CHRISTMAS, Al Riccio Photography

Inside Front Cover, CANDLELIGHT MAGIC,
Original painting by Donald Zolan
© Pemberton & Oakes—All Rights Reserved

Inside Back Cover, LAURIE AND THE CRÈCHE,
Original painting by Donald Zolan
© Pemberton & Oakes—All Rights Reserved

The First Snowfall

LaVerne P. Larson

When snowflakes start to tumble
In their first and merry flight,
It fills my heart with wonder,
For it is a lovely sight.

The air becomes a whirlpool
And goes dancing round and round
As these dainty, crystal charmers
Softly flutter to the ground.

They set my heart to dreaming
Of the days of long ago
When I gained a special joy
At the first white gown of snow.

I see each jolly snowman
And the giant slides we made,
The snow forts, and the frozen pond
Where all we children played.

As I watch the swirling flakes,
A magic spell is cast;
The first snowfall of winter
Is my mirror to the past.

PETTING FARM
Ann Arbor, Michigan
H.G. Ross/H. Armstrong Roberts

Christmas Came to Town

Lucille Crumley

Christmas came to our town
With its cold and wintry weather.
A myriad of snowflakes
Came floating down together.

They floated here and drifted there
With no design or limit,
Yet the scene was changing face
With every flying minute.

As if by some unheard command,
They all began to tumble
And wrap our little town in white
Just like a Christmas bundle.

The snowflakes hurried, scurried down
And swirled in ice delight.
When morning came, our little town
Was gift-wrapped in the night.

CANDLES IN THE WINDOW
Original Painting by Linda Nelson Stocks

©Linda Nelson Stocks 1990

The Snowman

Grace E. Easley

I laughed when I saw him,
 Who comically stood
With his bright eyes of coal
 And his gay mouth of wood.
His nose was a carrot,
 So pointed and thin,
And a deep dimple sat
 On the end of his chin.

Flat on the top
 Of his round, snowy head,
He wore a warm cap
 Of delectable red.
He carried a broom
 That was battered and brown,
And he gave a sly wink
 Like an oversize clown.

He stood by the fence
 Where a thick cedar grew,
The awesome attraction
 Of more than a few
Of the snowbirds who perched
 On a sheltering limb
And were quite evidently
 Bewildered by him.

I cannot be certain,
 But as I stood near,
I thought I saw just
 A slight twitch of his ear.
He seemed to be listening
 For something somewhere
That, however I tried,
 I could never quite hear.

And then from the valley
 I heard a glad shout
As a bell clanged, announcing
 That school had let out.
And from all directions
 The children appeared,
Glad that the snowman
 Had not disappeared.

They patted fresh snow
 On his arms and his cheeks,
Straightened his cap
 And his broom amid squeaks
Of childish enjoyment
 That touched even him,
And his wood mouth turned upward
 From smiling at them.

His coal eyes grew misty
 To watch how they pressed
Their curly heads close
 To his big snowy chest.
And was it the wind
 That I heard softly say,
"Oh, what a joy
 To watch children at play!"?

Country CHRONICLE

— Lansing Christman —

Christmas will always be Christmas, snow or no snow.

I remember as a child wishing with all my heart that we would have a white Christmas. At that time I lived in upstate New York. There, as the years passed, it was rare that snow did not fall on Christmas. When a snowless Christmas did occur, we referred to it as a "green" Christmas. As far as the ground was concerned, however, the fields and pastures were brown and sere. What green there was came from the evergreens—the pine and hemlock, the cedar and spruce—and the grass around the warm spring holes in the woods.

Now, having lived in upstate South Carolina for the past twenty-five years, a white Christmas is as rare as were those "green" Christmases in the Northeast. Here, in the foothills of the Blue Ridge Mountains, a green Christmas is typical—and truly green. The green is seen in the evergreens, some of our dooryards, and the fields sown with grain where the new crop is pushing up through the soil.

Whether we have a white or green Christmas does not matter to me. The basic emphasis is on the holy birth of the Christ Child in Bethlehem. North or south, east or west, a worshipful Christmas is Christ-centered. I can find the meaning of this holy day both in the churches and in the countryside—out in the hills or in the woods, along the brooks and streams, and even in my own dooryard. I hear the music of Christmas in the churches, and I can also hear it in the birdsongs just outside my window and in the woodland surrounding my home—the songs of the chickadees and cardinals, the bluebirds and house finches, the titmice and wrens.

Christmas is everywhere around us—white or green or brown—in what we see and hear, in what we feel deep within our hearts. Christmas will never change; it is in our souls. Christmas is a time to rejoice, to sense the intense spiritual meaning of this holy day when Christ is in our hearts and we have accepted Him as our Lord and Saviour.

So ring your bells and sing your carols, and have a worshipful, merry Christmas!

The author of two published books, Lansing Christman has been contributing to Ideals *for over twenty years. Mr. Christman has also been published in several American, foreign, and braille anthologies. He lives in rural South Carolina.*

Snow Scene

Georgia B. Adams

The snow is falling softly now
On every naked branch and bough;
Like lace, the flakes gently descend.
See how the roads that twist and bend

Have almost lost identity
Beneath this sparkling majesty;
The everlasting hills beyond
Their snow-white ermine capes have donned;

The mountains, regal in repose,
Release me from my daily woes;
On every naked branch and bough,
The snow is falling softly now.

WINTER LANDSCAPE
Superstock, Inc.

JACK FROST

Gabriel Setoun

The door was shut, as doors should be,
Before you went to bed last night;
Yet Jack Frost has got in, you see,
And left your window silver-white.

He must have waited till you slept;
And not a single word he spoke
But penciled o'er the panes and crept
Away again before you woke.

And now you cannot see the hills
Nor fields that stretch beyond the lane;
But there are fairer things than these:
His fingers traced on every pane

Rocks and castles towering high;
Hills and dales, and streams and fields;
And knights in armor riding by
With nodding plumes and shining shields;

And butterflies with gauzy wings;
And herds of cows and flocks of sheep;
And fruit and flowers and all the things
You see when you are sound asleep.

For, creeping softly underneath
The door when all the lights are out,
Jack Frost takes every breath you breathe
And knows the things you think about.

He paints them on the windowpane
In fairy lines with frozen steam;
And when you wake you see again
The lovely things you saw in dream.

The unique perspective of Russ Flint's artistic style has made him a favorite of Ideals *readers for many years. A resident of California and father of four, Russ Flint has illustrated a children's Bible and many other books.*

The Song of the Christmas Tree

Blanche Elizabeth Wade

Oho for the woods where I used to grow,
The home of the lonely owl and crow!
I spread my arms to shelter all
The creatures shy, both large and small.

I sang for joy to the friends I knew:
The sunshine, rain, and the sky so blue.
Oho for the forest! Oho for the hills!
Oho for the ripples of murmuring rills!
        Oho, sing I, oho!

Oho for the hall where I now hold sway,
The home of the happy children gay!
I spread my arms with gifts for all,
From father big to baby small.

I sing for joy to these hearts that glow—
Of manger bed and the Child we know.
Oho for the holly! Oho for the light!
Oho for the mistletoe's berries so white!
        Oho, sing I, oho!

A SLICE OF LIFE

Edgar A. Guest

Pa Did It

The train of cars that Santa brought is out of kilter now;
While Pa was showing how they went, he broke the spring somehow.
They used to run around a track—at least they did when he
Would let me take them in my hands an' wind 'em with a key.
I could 'a' had some fun with 'em, if only they would go,
But, gee! I never had a chance, for Pa enjoyed 'em so.

The automobile that I got that ran around the floor
Was lots of fun when it was new, but it won't go no more.
Pa wound it up for Uncle Jim to show him how it went,
An' when those two got through with it, the runnin' gear was bent,
An' now it doesn't go at all. I mustn't grumble though,
'Cause while it was in shape to run, my Pa enjoyed it so.

I've got my blocks as good as new; my mitts are perfect yet;
Although the snow is on the ground, I haven't got 'em wet.
I've taken care of everything that Santa brought to me
Except the toys that run about when wound up with a key.
But next year you can bet I won't make any such mistake;
I'm going to ask for toys an' things that my Pa cannot break.

Edgar A. Guest began his illustrious career in 1895 at the age of fourteen when his work first appeared in the Detroit Free Press. *His column was syndicated in over 300 newspapers, and he became known as "The Poet of the People."*

Growing Up at Christmastime

Christie Craig

ell me the truth, Mama!"
With the dollar bill still crunched in my hand, I looked down at my seven-year-old daughter and knew I'd been caught red-handed. There was no escaping it. I was going to have to tell Nina the truth. It would hurt her, no doubt; but for the first time I realized it was going to hurt me more.

"There's not a tooth fairy, is there?" she asked and sat up stiffly in bed.

I unwrinkled the dollar in my hand. This wasn't the question I'd dreaded, but it was December, and I knew where this conversation would lead.

As I pondered the right words, I remembered my father on the Christmas Eve I'd confronted him with my discovery of all the toys hidden in the attic. His words had been so loving, so tender; but for the first time I understood that misty look in his eyes.

"No, there isn't a tooth fairy," I said softly and brushed back her bangs.

She crossed her arms and stared down at the rumpled quilt on her bed. I could almost hear the questions ticking away in her mind. I had the strangest urge to cuddle her close as I had when she was an infant. It was the same strange feeling I'd experienced when she first started walking and, more recently, when she started school.

"What about Santa? Is he real or do you bring the gifts?" she demanded.

I swallowed the lump in my throat and joined her on the bed. In that moment I remembered all the Christmas mornings of her young life and the look of awe that played across her face when she opened her gifts from Santa. I would miss those magical times.

Studying the imaginary lint on my housecoat, I considered trying to convince her that this legend was true. But when I looked into her face, I knew what I had to do.

I reached for her hand. Then in the gentlest of words I gave her the same talk my father

Meeting my daughter's gaze, I watched as she gave up another little piece of her childhood. It wasn't easy for either of us, but neither were her first steps or her first week of school.

had given me twenty years ago. The one about Santa being a spirit that lives on in our traditions of love and gifts. I ended my speech the same way my father had ended his, reminding her of the real meaning of Christmas: the celebration of the Christ Child's birth.

Meeting my daughter's gaze, I watched as she gave up another little piece of her childhood. It wasn't easy for either of us, but neither were her first steps or her first week of school. After she'd dressed for school, I fed her breakfast and sent her to the bus stop. Standing by the window, I gazed at her chatting with her friends. I wanted to stand with her, but only the week before she'd told me she was a big girl and requested I stay behind.

That evening I told my husband about the conversation. At dinner, she brought up the subject. "It makes me very sad and yet happy at the same time," Nina explained as she moved her peas around her plate. "Sad because now that I know Santa isn't real, I feel like I've lost a friend. And happy because . . ." she glanced up at us with a gleam of mischief in her eyes, "now I know I really don't have to be good all year long for Santa to bring me gifts." She smiled, and we laughed. We understood her mixture of emotions. As parents, we too felt sadness mixed with happiness at the realization that our little girl was growing up.

Readers' Reflections

Editor's Note: Readers are invited to submit unpublished, original poetry for possible publication in future issues of Ideals. *Please send copies only; manuscripts will not be returned. Writers receive $10 for each published submission. Send material to "Readers' Reflections," Ideals Publications Inc., P.O. Box 148000, Nashville, TN 37214-8000.*

The Greatest Gift

On a cold and silent night
   Two thousand years ago,
The greatest gift man ever knew
   God sent to earth below.

Angels came from heaven
   With a glorious song of cheer.
To shepherds in a quiet field
   They said, "Please, have no fear.

"For in a nearby stable
   A Saviour you will find—

The One the Lord has promised,
   The One who'll save mankind."

And so the shepherds hurried off
   To find the King of Kings;
And when they finally found Him,
   Their hearts began to sing.

For this Baby in the manger
   Was sent from God above.
He came to bring us joy and hope
   And teach us how to love.

Cheryl R. Smith
Borden, Indiana

Christmas

Christmas is a time
   for giving,
A time for love
   and joyous living,

For glistening splendor
   and lots of laughter,
Making happy memories
   forever after.

But with all the glitter,
   fun, and mirth,
Let's not forget
   the Christ Child's birth,

And the peace
   that was meant to be.
Dear Lord,
   let it begin with me,

And may it spread
   throughout the earth
In celebration of
   our Saviour's birth.

Anna Beth Minyard
Edinburg, Texas

Welcome to Bethlehem

I heard the knock and opened up—
A foolish thing to do—
I held the door but just ajar
To let no travelers through.

Before I spoke, my wife came by
And briskly had her say:
"You are too late; there is no room."
Then her voice trailed away.

"Perhaps the stable in the back?"
She whispered in my ear,
And as I led them there I saw
The woman's time was near.

I heaped some straw for makeshift beds
And fed the donkey hay.
Then back I went to mind the inn,
But my wife chose to stay.

Before too long she came to me
And said the strangest thing:
"With the Child's birth the stable seems
A palace for a king!"

They were not there for very long.
Still many came to see
The little Princeling holding court
Upon His mother's knee.

Ethel Dietrich
Lewisville, Texas

Shepherds' Christmas Sequel

I wonder if in later years
The shepherds ever saw
The Lamb of God they worshipped once
As He lay on the straw.

But intervening years were long
With not a sight of Him.
For thirty years their hearts still hoped,
Some eyes now growing dim.

The mem'ry of that glorious night
Was ever crystal clear—
How angels and the guiding star
Brought heaven very near.

And, best of all, they Jesus saw,
So bright-eyed and so small,
So fresh from God, so innocent—
He seemed to be for all.

Years move on, and then I see
Young Jesus in His prime
As He stops by that shepherds' field
To visit for a time.

My mind's eye sees Him hug these men.
The dim eyes, how they shine!
For now their Shepherd they embrace,
Our precious Lord divine.

Virginia R. Hendrick
Flint, Michigan

SAGUAROS IN THE SNOW. Dick Dietrich Photography.

Christmas
on the
Rio Grande

Bob Rose

I grew up with snow and ice,
Apple cider laced with spice,
Caroling on coldest nights
While pine trees glowed with twinkling lights.

Now I live on the Rio Grande—
Cactus plants and lots of sand,
Palm trees pointing to the sky,
And warm gulf breezes blowing by.

The malls are trying hard to show
What things look like when heaped with snow.
Christmas trees are hard to find
(And mostly the synthetic kind).

I didn't know how I would feel
Since everything seemed so unreal
When Christmas season was at hand
While I lived on the Rio Grande.

But then it came to me one day
That Christmas wasn't just for play,
For Santa Claus and snow and trees,
And incidentals such as these.

My mind went back through time and space
And landed in a distant place

Where Christ was born, in Bethlehem,
A place not unlike where I am.

I saw no pines with twinkling lights,
No fields of snow or frosty nights,
No holly wreaths or mistletoe,
No "Rudolph" with his nose aglow.

I saw a barren, desert land
With palm trees rising from the sand.
The sun beat down and warmed the breeze
That moved the sand and bent the trees.

I felt the warmth upon my face
And saw the beauty of the place.
My vision made me realize
I must view Christmas though new eyes.

The things that make our season bright
Are far removed from Christmas night.
We should recall the humble birth,
The night that God came down to earth.

My thoughts have made it very clear:
The season's blessings all are here.
With palm trees and the desert sand,
It's Christmas on the Rio Grande.

TRAVELER'S Diary

Lisa C. Thompson

A TOUR OF THE HISTORIC DISTRICT. Photograph courtesy of the Bethlehem Tourism Authority, Bethlehem, Pennsylvania.

BETHLEHEM, PENNSYLVANIA

Historic Moravian Community

The first thing nighttime visitors notice about the charming Moravian community that is Bethlehem, Pennsylvania, is the lights. Thousands of white lights shine in the windows of homes and shops all over the small city and make it look like a winter wonderland. Hundreds of miniature Christmas trees decorate the lampposts throughout the downtown area of renovated Victorian buildings. The unique Moravian star, a twenty-six-pointed star made of parchment that is lighted from within, is visible all over the city. High atop South Mountain, the Star of Bethlehem—mounted on a ninety-one-foot-tower and visible for twenty miles—summons people from near and far to the "Christmas City."

The religious significance of the season is not lost to commercialism in Bethlehem, Pennsylvania, which was named by its Moravian settlers at a Christmas Eve service in 1741. Special church services such as the Moravian Love Feast and the Messiah Sing-a-long bring visitors from the gift shops into the churches. The live nativity scene on the Court House Square features solemn actors, furry animals, and an inspiring narrative. Candles are lit, one each week, on the large Advent wreaths hanging on the Hill to Hill Bridge to indicate the approach of Christmas Day. The celebration of the birth of Christ is evident in every event in Bethlehem.

Visitors can visit the Bethlehem of yesteryear with horse-drawn carriage rides or walking tours of historic Bethlehem, a city founded by Moravian missionaries primarily from Germany who sought to spread the Good News to the people of the New World. Some visitors choose the Lantern Light Tour, a nighttime tour of the historic district complete with guides in traditional Moravian garb. The tours often include a visit to the Moravian Museum located in the Gemeinhaus, which was built in 1741 and is the oldest building in Bethlehem. Exhibits are arranged in rooms throughout the building to interpret authentically the life and surroundings of the early Moravians, a group of people dedicated to religious life, handicrafts, and the cultivation of music. Displays throughout the log-structured building feature Early Moravian furniture, clocks, silver, musical instruments, religious art, and needlework. The Fire Engine Annex houses two original eighteenth-century, hand-drawn fire engines.

MORAVIAN HERITAGE. Photograph courtesy of the Bethlehem Tourism Authority, Bethlehem, Pennsylvania.

Several area churches host a Christmas Putz, an elaborate nativity scene that features antique figurines set in a miniature landscape of moss, evergreen trees, rocks, and driftwood. The scene is narrated with the story of Christ's birth while strategic lighting highlights the different areas of the putz. The putz, a word that comes from the German *putzen* which means "to decorate," is a tradition borrowed from Germany. Audience members can often feast on Moravian sugar cake and coffee following the presentation.

Candles and candlemaking also play an important role in the Christmas City's festivities. The early Moravians believed that beeswax candles symbolized the purity of Christ, and during a special Christmas service in 1747, they passed out the candles to worshippers. Today members of the Moravian Church still mold, trim, and distribute beeswax candles for their Christmas vigils, and thousands more are made by other area churches and shops. Beeswax candlemaking demonstrations can be seen all over the city during the Christmas season.

Visitors to Bethlehem also enjoy a special festival called Christkindlmarkt, which features handmade crafts including pottery, woven textiles, jewelry, and Christmas ornaments; entertainment such as caroling choirs, live organ music, jugglers, and other performers; and food vendors which specialize in German, Austrian, and Pennsylvania Dutch food. The festival is based on the medieval German Christmas markets where the city and country people gathered together to shop and celebrate the season. Children can escape to an imaginary Black Forest in a special section designed just for them called Dreamland, which features a life-size gingerbread house, petting zoo, and Kindermarkt, a shopping area just for kids where they can buy inexpensive holiday gifts.

A journey to Bethlehem, Pennsylvania, this Christmas will remind you of the true spirit of this holy season as you learn more about the Moravian missionaries who journeyed to America centuries ago. To find this charming city twinkling in the Lehigh Valley of southern Pennsylvania, just follow the star in the sky.

No Room

Kay Hoffman

"No room," the busy innkeeper said
But offered them the stable shed;
With no more thought of their request,
He hurried on to serve his guests.

The little town was deep in sleep;
None heard the sound of shepherds' feet
Or saw the star of wondrous ray
That led to where the Christ Child lay.

Only the shepherds and wise men came
Offering praises to His name;
The little Saviour born for all
Lay in a humble manger stall.

Close to the stable, low and dim,
The guests inside the crowded inn,
With shuttered door and shades drawn tight,
Knew naught of what transpired that night.

As keeper of my little inn,
Oh, I must wait and watch for Him
Lest He would come tonight and find
No room within this heart of mine.

NO ROOM IN THE INN
Original painting by Robert Heuel

The Mission to Gabriel and Annunciation

And in the sixth month the angel Gabriel was sent
from God unto a city of Galilee, named Nazareth,
To a virgin espoused to a man whose name was Joseph,
of the house of David; and the virgin's name was Mary.
And the angel came in unto her, and said,
Hail, thou that art highly favoured, the Lord is with thee:
blessed art thou among women.
And the angel said unto her, Fear not, Mary:
for thou hast found favour with God.
And, behold, thou shalt conceive in thy womb,
and bring forth a son, and shalt call his name
JESUS.
Then said Mary unto the angel,
How shall this be, seeing I know not a man?
And the angel answered and said unto her,
The Holy Ghost shall come upon thee,
and the power of the Highest shall overshadow thee:
therefore also that holy thing
which shall be born of thee shall be called the Son of God.
And Mary said,
Behold the handmaid of the Lord;
be it unto me according to thy word.

Luke 1:26-28, 30-31, 34-35, 38

The Visitation

And Mary arose in those days,
and went into the hill country with haste,
into a city of Juda;
And entered into the house of Zacharias,
and saluted Elisabeth.
And it came to pass, that, when Elisabeth heard
the salutation of Mary,
the babe leaped in her womb; and
Elisabeth was filled with the Holy Ghost:
And she spake out with a loud voice, and said,
Blessed art thou among women, and
blessed is the fruit of thy womb.
For, lo, as soon as the voice of thy salutation sounded
in mine ears, the babe leaped in my womb for joy.
And blessed is she that believed:
for there shall be a performance of those things
which were told her from the Lord.
And Mary said,
My soul doth magnify the Lord,
And my spirit hath rejoiced in God my Saviour.

Luke 1:39-42, 44-47

THE VISITATION
Giotto di Bondone (1266?–1337)
Fresco in Scrovegni Chapel, Padua, Italy
Scala/Art Resource, New York

The Nativity

nd she brought forth her firstborn son,
and wrapped him in swaddling clothes,
and laid him in a manger;
because there was no room for them in the inn.
And there were in the same country shepherds
abiding in the field, keeping watch over their flock by night.
And, lo, the angel of the Lord came upon them,
and the glory of the Lord shone round about them:
and they were sore afraid.
And the angel said unto them, Fear not:
for, behold, I bring you good tidings of great joy,
which shall be to all people.
For unto you is born this day in the city of David
a Saviour, which is Christ the Lord.
And suddenly there was with the angel a multitude
of the heavenly host praising God, and saying,
Glory to God in the highest,
and on earth peace, good will toward men.

Luke 2:7-11, 13-14

The Adoration of the Magi

ow when Jesus was born in Bethlehem of Judæa
in the days of Herod the king,
behold, there came wise men
from the east to Jerusalem,
Saying,
Where is he that is born King of the Jews?
for we have seen his star in the east,
and are come to worship him.
When they saw the star,
they rejoiced with exceeding great joy.
And when they were come into the house,
they saw the young child with Mary his mother,
and fell down, and worshipped him:
and when they had opened their treasures,
they presented unto him gifts;
gold, and frankincense, and myrrh.

Matthew 2:1-2, 10-11

The Presentation in the Temple

And when the days of her purification
according to the law of Moses were accomplished,
they brought him to Jerusalem,
to present him to the Lord;
And, behold, there was a man in Jerusalem,
whose name was Simeon;
and the same man was just and devout,
waiting for the consolation of Israel:
and the Holy Ghost was upon him.
And it was revealed unto him by the Holy Ghost,
that he should not see death,
before he had seen the Lord's Christ.
And he came by the Spirit into the temple:
and when the parents brought in the child Jesus,
to do for him after the custom of the law,
Then took he him up in his arms, and blessed God, and said,
Lord, now lettest thou thy servant depart in peace,
according to thy word:
For mine eyes have seen thy salvation,
Which thou hast prepared before the face of all people;
A light to lighten the Gentiles,
and the glory of thy people Israel.

Luke 2:22, 25-32

The Flight into Egypt

And when they were departed,
behold, the angel of the Lord
appeareth to Joseph in a dream, saying,
Arise, and take the young child and his mother,
and flee into Egypt,
and be thou there until I bring thee word:
for Herod will seek the young child to destroy him.
When he arose, he took the young child and his mother
by night, and departed into Egypt:
And was there until the death of Herod:
that it might be fulfilled which was spoken of the Lord
by the prophet, saying,
Out of Egypt have I called my son.

Matthew 2:13-15

The Shepherds Had an Angel

Christina G. Rossetti

The shepherds had an angel;
　　The wise men had a star.
But what have I, a little child,
　　To guide me home from far,
Where glad stars sing together
　　And singing angels are?

Lord Jesus is my Guardian,
　　So I can nothing lack;
The lambs lie in His bosom
　　Along life's dangerous track.
The willful lambs that go astray,
　　He, bleeding, brings them back.

Those shepherds through the lonely night
　　Sat watching by their sheep
Until they saw the heav'nly host
　　Who neither tire nor sleep,
All singing "Glory, glory"
　　In festival they keep.

Christ watches me, His little lamb,
　　Cares for me day and night,
That I may be His own in heav'n;
　　So angels clad in white
Shall sing their "Glory, glory"
　　For my sake in the height.

Lord, bring me nearer day by day
　　Till I my voice unite
And sing my "Glory, glory"
　　With angels clad in white.
All glory, glory, given to Thee,
　　Through all the heav'nly height.

41

COLLECTOR'S CORNER

Lisa C. Thompson

THE HOLY FAMILY. A traditional crèche figurine.

CRÈCHES
Nativity Scenes

Family traditions run deep at Christmastime. One tradition observed in homes all around the world is that of setting up the crèche in its place of honor—on the mantel, the Christmas tree skirt, or the coffee table—as a visual reminder of the true meaning of this joyous holiday. Children stare in awe at the figures and desperately try to keep from playing with them, quite a feat for many curious fingers. As mothers and fathers dash through the

living room in the chaos of preparing for the big day, the crèche catches their eye; and they stop for a moment to whisper a prayer. The crèche becomes a powerful, though silent, symbol of the greatest love of all time.

The word crèche is French for crib and symbolizes a tradition that dates back to 1223 to the small village of Greccio, Italy. One night not long before Christmas, St. Francis of Assisi and his followers were traveling through the coun-

42

tryside on their way to Greccio. St. Francis had been pondering a way to bring the message of Christ's birth to everyone in a special, symbolic way. As St. Francis traveled the lonely, country road, he saw shepherds resting in a nearby field. The sight reminded him of the shepherds to whom the angel had appeared that night long ago with good tidings of great joy. It spurred his imagination; and on Christmas Eve, he gave a special gift to the people of Greccio: St. Francis recreated the holy scene of the nativity right before their eyes, complete with a manger, donkey and ox, Mary and Joseph, and the baby Jesus.

Soon word spread of that special night in Greccio, and other towns began creating their own crèche scenes. By the eighteenth century, the crèches, called *presepi* in Italy, had become an established and respected art form in Naples. Artists combined their talents of sculpture, painting, and scenic design to produce elaborate scenes with intricate details such as authentic clothes of the Neapolitan period, tiny baskets of wax fruit, and even bejeweled magi. Members of the upperclasses began setting up crèches in their own homes and establishing lasting family traditions. One notable Baroque Neopolitan crèche was that of King Charles III of Naples; his crèche numbered almost 6,000 pieces.

Notable crèche exhibits

ETHNIC CRÈCHE. Superstock, Inc.

in the United States include *The Adoration of Angels* at the Metropolitan Museum of Art, which features angels sweeping down a tree to hover over the Holy Family. The crèche figures were donated by Lynn Hines Howard, who spent more than thirty years collecting the pieces. The Boston Museum of Fine Arts features a beautiful ceramic crèche made by an eighteenth century Venetian sculptor as well as a fifteenth-century glazed terracotta crèche by Luca della Robbia. Just as the people of Greccio journeyed to see the first crèche from St. Francis, so do the people of America today journey to see special crèche exhibits across the country.

The gift of the crèche from St. Francis has brought joy and understanding to millions of people around the world ever since he first created it that enchanted evening in Greccio, Italy.

CROSS-STITCH CRÈCHE. John David Harper/New England Stock Photo.

It has more than fulfilled his desire to convey the message of the Christmas story in a special, symbolic way. Crèche collectors may delight in the tiny details or artistic flair of their crèche pieces, but more important is the contemplative, prayerful attitude and feelings that the miniature displays invoke. Perhaps this year we should forgo the tissue, boxes, and packing crates and leave the crèche standing in its place of honor throughout the year as a symbol of the meaning of Christmas in our daily lives.

Christmas Joy

Reverend J. Harold Gwynne

The angel herald spoke of joy—
God's gift to humankind—
And humble shepherds quickly came,
Incarnate joy to find.

The wise men, guided by the star,
Rejoiced with purest joy;
Their journey led them where they found
The Mother and her Boy!

And now this blessed Christmas joy
Is known throughout the earth,
As joyful people everywhere
Observe the Christ Child's birth.

And still the joy of Christmas comes
To fill our hearts with cheer;
This joy of which the angels sang
Grows sweeter every year.

This Christmas joy within our hearts
Is deep and full and free;
It is the spirit of our Lord,
The Man of Galilee.

ROCKEFELLER CENTER
New York, New York
R. Krubner/H. Armstrong Roberts

THROUGH MY WINDOW

Pamela Kennedy

Art by Russ Flint

THE SPIRIT OF THE CRÈCHE

It might have been all the Christmas issues of the magazines in the check-out lines at the grocery store, or perhaps it was the mall decorations that went up right after Halloween, but I decided that for once in our lives we would have a "perfect" Christmas. I would plan and schedule and prepare so we would eliminate that last minute chaos so typical of the holiday. We would have bountiful evergreens and sweet, spicy baked goods and warm evenings by the fire with Christmas carols playing in the background. And so I diligently set about to make it happen.

Most things were moving along according to plan, and my checklists were almost all checked— until the weekend we were to get the tree. My son and daughter were invited to a professional hockey game, and my husband got stuck with an extra project at work, so I ended up at the tree lot trying to find the perfect tree alone.

After hours of indecision and dozens of pokes and prickles, I chose a chubby fir. The verdict at home that evening was not as enthusiastic as I had hoped. "Too fat," offered my daughter. "Too short," complained my son. "Well, it has character," observed my tired husband.

"It will look perfect when it's decorated," I suggested. We hauled out the boxes of decorations. "You know what would be really lovely? Let's build a fire in the fireplace and play carols as we decorate the tree!" I offered. I located the Christmas tapes while my husband and son started building the fire. The music started, but something was terribly wrong. The Mormon Tabernacle Choir sounded like it was on tranquilizers as "Joy to the World" quivered from the speakers in a flat drawl.

"The heat last summer must have stretched the tapes or something," my husband said. I tried another tape, but the results were the same.

"Maybe it's the player. Let's try them in the car and see if they sound the same."

We were sitting in the driveway listening to atonal Christmas carols when the children came dashing out of the house screaming, "Dad! Mom! Hurry, the fireplace is all smoky!"

We ran inside to the shriek of the smoke alarm as billows of smoke poured from the fireplace. "Open the flue!" shouted my husband as he fanned his way through the bluish air.

Later that evening, after the children were tucked in bed and the house was somewhat aired out, I sat going through a box of Christmas ornaments. Due to the fire alert, we had never gotten around to decorating the tree, and I had the ominous feeling that Christmas was beginning to take on its usual chaotic nature. I was a week behind on my baking schedule, two boxes of unaddressed cards mocked me from the top of the desk, and the number of shopping days left till Christmas was quickly diminishing. What happened to all my good intentions?

In the bottom of the box I found the crèche in a plastic bag. Clearing a place atop the coffee table, I began to arrange the pieces. As I stood the shepherds beside the stable door, my husband entered the room bearing two cups of coffee.

"Is this a private Christmas party, or can I join you?"

I smiled at him and patted the floor next to where I was sitting. Silently, we situated sheep and donkeys, wise men and angels. Looking at the quiet, peaceful expression on the ceramic Mary, I sighed wistfully.

"What was that all about?" he asked.

"Oh," I replied. "It just isn't working out the way I'd planned."

"What isn't?" He rested his elbow on the table and looked at me.

"Christmas," I answered. "I wanted it to be perfect and lovely and not all chaotic and confused and rushed this year. I thought I could make it work out that way if I planned everything, but crazy, unexpected things just keep happening and . . ." I looked at him with tears swimming in my eyes.

Thoughtfully, he picked up the figure of Joseph and turned him around. "I'll bet that's how he felt too," he said.

I was puzzled. "What?"

"Well, here he was all set to get married, then, wham! Mary hits him with the news that she's going to have the Son of God. And look at these guys." He picked up a shepherd in each hand. "There they were, having a nice, quiet night on the hillside when—"Halleluia in the Highest!"— tons of angels start shouting at them! And what about these fellows?" He lined the magi in a row. "Minding their own business in Persia or someplace, making star charts, and all of a sudden they have to pack up their camels and head out west! And when they get there, they find out they're in the wrong place and the king they're looking for is only a toddler. Boy, did their plans get changed."

I giggled at his dramatics.

"But let's not forget Mary here. She didn't even get to spend Christmas at home! I'd be willing to bet that wasn't in her plan!" He leaned over and pulled me towards him in a hug. "You know what?"

"What?"

"Christmas isn't so much about planning and schedules and organizing stuff as it is about welcoming the unexpected surprises of life."

We sat there for a long time that evening, and I still recall it as one of my favorite Christmas memories. I think of it each December when my plans get interrupted. I think of it when I begin to feel overwhelmed with all the holiday entertaining and I become discouraged about losing "the true meaning of Christmas." But I especially think of it each time I tuck the tiny baby Jesus in his ceramic crib. Because it is then I recall with gratitude how God interrupted the world one night almost two thousand years ago and changed all our plans forever.

Pamela Kennedy is a free-lance writer of short stories, articles, essays, and children's books. Wife of a naval officer and mother of three children, she has made her home on both U.S. coasts and currently resides in Honolulu, Hawaii. She draws her material from her own experiences and memories, adding bits of her imagination to create a story or mood.

The Secret of the Bullfinch

Barbara Craig

At a quaint German inn near the Austrian border, the bullfinch perched in its cage in the dining room, where it regularly serenaded customers.

One warm, spring morning in 1854, only one guest sat in the dining room, but he was an impressive personage indeed. His name was Ludwig Eck, the concertmaster of the Berlin Cathedral Choir.

Eck had been enjoying a quiet breakfast, at least, until the bird chirped its song. As the melody filled the air, a bewildered expression covered his face.

"Shall I remove the bird cage?" asked the waiter, who had noticed Eck's puzzled look.

"No," said the concertmaster, and in an effort to explain, he continued, "It's the song the bird is singing. That song has been on my mind for so long, I thought for a moment I was humming it to myself." Seven years earlier, Eck had been asked by officials of his celebrated choral group to find the composer of the tune.

"The emperor himself has requested that the person who wrote the song be found," explained the concertmaster. "The song has no name above it in our hymn book, but it has become a great favorite of the emperor. He wants to meet the person who wrote it."

For seven long years, Eck had searched for the composer of the emperor's favorite hymn.

He had traveled to all corners of Germany and to nearby countries in his quest. He had investigated every rumor and even rumors of rumors about the song. His search had caused him to neglect his work as concertmaster, but he had never yet come close to finding who wrote the tune.

"Where did you get that bird?" Eck asked the waiter. He did not know but offered to check with the owner of the inn. The waiter was gone no more than five minutes, but to Eck it seemed an eternity. The concertmaster impatiently strummed his fingers on the table and ignored the breakfast in front of him. Deep down, he sensed his search would soon be over.

The bullfinch came from a Felix Gruber, a student at St. Peter's Abbey across the border in Austria, the waiter told Eck when he returned. "Felix trained it to sing the song. Students at the abbey often train birds to sing and then sell them."

Within the hour, Eck was on his way to the abbey, which was located near Salzburg.

The abbot at St. Peter's couldn't believe that one of his students trained the bird. "We have disciplined students for doing such a thing. Here, we feel it is a cruel practice to cage a bird and deprive one of God's creatures of its freedom."

Nevertheless, the concertmaster insisted on speaking to Felix Gruber. "I am on my emperor's business," he said.

A few minutes later, the youth, who was about fifteen, stood in the abbot's office. "Yes sir," he said with reluctance, eyeing the abbot nervously as he did, "I trained the bullfinch to sing the song."

"Who taught you the song?"

"My father," said the youth.

"And where did he learn it?" Eck asked. The distinguished concertmaster almost leapt for joy when he heard the answer.

"My father," said the young man with a trace of pride, "wrote the music, and his friend wrote the words."

Felix was not disciplined for training the bullfinch, even though he had violated the school's rules. The abbot was in a forgiving mood. After all, it wasn't every day he had an emissary of the Emperor of Germany in his office.

The following week, Eck, accompanied by young Gruber, arrived in the village of Hallein, where the student's father was the organist at the local church.

Franz Gruber acknowledged his part in the creation of the song. "It happened many years ago—on Christmas Eve in 1818, to be exact. At the time I was the organist at St. Nicholas Church in Oberndorf. The organ broke down, and for a while it seemed we would not have any music at our Christmas service.

"Father Joseph Mohr, who is dead now, had composed a poem about the birth of Christ. At his request, I put music to the words and performed it on my guitar at the Christmas mass.

"We never expected to play the song again, but it became quite popular. People began singing it at Christmas in villages all over the Tyrolean Mountains."

Gruber didn't realize just how far the popularity of their song had spread. "Father Mohr and I knew it was a great favorite where we lived. We were unaware our music had traveled to distant lands."

The church organist was invited to meet the emperor of Germany. "He's been waiting a long time to meet the person who created 'The Song from Heaven,'" Eck said to Gruber.

"'The Song from Heaven'?" Gruber was puzzled.

"That is what we call your song in Germany," said the concertmaster. "What do you call your song here?"

"We call it what Father Mohr called it when he wrote his poem," said Gruber. "'Silent Night.'"

Silent night, holy night;
Shepherds quake at the sight.
Glories stream from heaven afar;
Heav'nly hosts sing Alleluia.
Christ the Saviour is born;
Christ the Saviour is born.

Silent night, holy night;
Son of God, love's pure light;
Radiant beams from Thy holy face,
With the dawn of redeeming grace.
Jesus, Lord, at Thy birth;
Jesus, Lord, at Thy birth.

Silent night, holy night;
Wondrous Star, lend thy light;
With the angels let us sing,
Alleluia to our King;
Christ the Saviour is born;
Christ the Saviour is born.

50 YEARS AGO

MARY MARTIN, VOCALIST. Archive Photos.

Soldiers Go for Bach

USO-Camp Shows, a participating service of the National War Fund, is today one of the most active concert-booking agents in the world. Working closely with the War Department, it is sending classical music to members of the American armed forces fighting on every battlefront.

Certainly a new era in concert bookings has dawned when jungle airstrips, South Pacific foxholes, and submarine decks under stress of war become concert platforms; and when top-flight concert artists, accustomed to the cotton-wool protection given to rare jewels, leave temperament behind to share the discomforts and dangers facing our soldiers.

An American concert hall would pay about $4,500 per concert for the average show put on for soldiers and sailors by the musicians now touring

the war theaters through Camp Shows and the War Department's Special Services.

War was never like this, is what the soldiers and sailors say. Jascha Heifetz, standing under a narrow tin roof, plays Saint-Saëns's "Rondo Capriccioso" in a jungle rainstorm before drenched G. I. Coast Artillerymen. Yehudi Menuhin, accompanied by a Seabee on a tinpanny upright piano and garbed in a turtleneck sweater, slacks and sneakers, plays Novocek's "Perpetual Motion" for Aleutian Island fliers who have just engaged the enemy.

Heifetz and Menuhin are only two of the "big names" who are canceling their scheduled and profitable professional concert tours, whenever they are called, to go out for USO-Camp Shows' Concert Division. They are only a fraction of the several hundred professional musicians who are taking concert music to men in the armed forces.

Gino Baldini, prominent in New York's music world for many years, is the dynamic director of this ambitious project for sending concerts and concert artists overseas. The Concert Division is supplying the musical talent—instrumentalists, vocalists, dancers—for more than 100 professional concerts a month in army camps and naval posts in the United States. At all times, he has between thirty and forty artists overseas who are giving two and three daily concerts, in addition to extemporaneous bedside recitals in hospitals, and nightcap recitals at tent and barrack doors.

At first USO-Camp Shows doubted that "highbrow" music would go over with the soldiers, who would, they believed, prefer light comedy and popular music, if any. But the first pioneer concerts by "highbrow" performers proved how wrong was this original belief.

These concert artists are playing and singing and dancing before thousands of soldiers who never before went to concerts, and who never before have seen "live" concert artists—or conspicuously wanted to see them. They are playing for many boys who never have seen some of the musical instruments.

When the concert artists first went out to the army camps, they felt that they should not play "over the heads" of their soldier-audiences and made up programs of popular, encore-type numbers. After a concert by one famous artist, a delegation of soldiers visited him.

"Do you play the things you played tonight before your Carnegie Hall audiences?" they asked.

The artist had to admit that he didn't, and he reported his calling-down to the USO-Camp Shows' Concert Division. Since that time, all the concert artists have given "Carnegie Hall concerts" everywhere they have appeared. They let the boys ask, as encores, for whatever popular numbers they want to hear.

These requests are always the same, whether the artist's medium is the voice, an instrument, or a piano. They ask for Schubert's "Ave Maria," Malotte's "The Lord's Prayer," the "Toreador Song" from Carmen with Rimsky-Korsakoff's "Flight of the Bumble Bee" and "Old Man River." Stephen Foster's songs and Negro spirituals are permanent soldier favorites.

USO's Concert Division knew that in sending concert artists abroad, the artists would sometimes have to dispense with their usual expert accompaniment, for pianos would not always be a part of military equipment. They concluded that an accordion would be the most reliable portable equipment and the Division has included an accordionist in as many concert tours as possible.

Folding organs, that many camp chaplains have learned to use, have pinch-hit on many occasions for a piano. Many Special Service G. I. companies playing overseas have mini-pianos and often graciously lend these. But after a bouncing trip over jungle roads to an advanced outpost, the pianos are pretty much off key when they arrive at their destination. On one trip, Heifetz took along a spinet for his accompaniment.

Concert artists must abandon all hope of comfortable living and comfortable traveling when they leave home shores for the Fijis, the Tongas, Cook and Society Islands, and all of the other isolated mid-ocean spots where American soldiers are to be found.

Means of transportation used by the artists to get from place to place are extremely informal. They hitch rides in anything that can move. One day, in the South Pacific, Earl Wrightson, baritone, and his fellow artists hitched in six different conveyances to get to their concert date—a jeep, an amphibious tank, a PT boat, a weapons carrier, a bomber, and a command car. One unit in the Port Darwin region of Australia borrowed an Army truck and a compass and drove themselves—"so the Army wouldn't have to be bothered about us."

Many people believe that these G. I. concerts are creating vast new audiences for tomorrow. Hundreds of soldiers, they reason, who never before were exposed to "good" music, are finding that they like it. These same soldiers, they say, will demand classical pieces when they come home.

Originally printed in The Christian Science Monitor Magazine, *December 9, 1944.*

Keeping Christmas

Henry van Dyke

It is a good thing to observe Christmas Day. The mere marking of times and seasons, when men agree to stop work and make merry together, is a wise and wholesome custom. It helps one to feel the supremacy of the common life over the individual life. It reminds a man to set his own little watch, now and then, by the great clock of humanity which runs on sun time.

But there is a better thing than the observance of Christmas Day, and that is keeping Christmas.

Are you willing to forget what you have done for other people and to remember what other people have done for you; to ignore what the world owes you and to think what you owe the world; to put your rights in the background and your duties in the middle distance and your chances to do a little more than your duty in the foreground; to see that your fellow men are just as real as you are and try to look behind their faces to their hearts, hungry for joy; to own that probably the only good reason for your existence is not what you are going to get out of life but what you are going to give to life; to close your book of complaints against the management of the universe and look around you for a place where you can sow a few seeds of happiness—are you willing to do these things for even a day? Then you can keep Christmas.

Are you willing to stoop down and consider the needs and desires of little children; to remember the weakness and loneliness of people who are growing old; to stop asking how much your friends love you, and ask yourself whether you love them enough; to bear in mind the things that other people have to bear on their hearts; to try to understand what those who live in the same house with you really want, without waiting for them to tell you; to trim your lamp so that it will give more light and less smoke; and to carry it in front so that your shadow will fall behind you; to make a grave for your ugly thoughts and a garden for your kind feelings with the gate open—are you willing to do these things even for a day? Then you can keep Christmas.

Are you willing to believe that love is the strongest thing in the world—stronger than hate, stronger than death—and that the blessed life which began in Bethlehem nineteen hundred years ago is the image and brightness of Eternal Love? Then you can keep Christmas.

And if you keep it for a day, why not always? But you can never keep it alone.

Lisa C. Thompson

Henry van Dyke
Clergyman and Author

The religious writings and poetry of Henry van Dyke have made him a favorite of the American people for decades. In his most popular novels, *The Story of the Other Wise Man* and *The First Christmas Tree*, van Dyke crafted inspiring stories based on Biblical teachings that bring the message of Christmas into our homes and hearts.

Henry van Dyke was born on November 10, 1852, in Germantown, Pennsylvania, the son of Henry Jackson van Dyke and Henrietta (Ashmead) van Dyke. The elder van Dyke was pastor of the First Presbyterian Church, a religious tie that would influence young Henry for the rest of his life. When Henry was just one year old, his father accepted a new appointment and moved the family to Brooklyn, New York, where van Dyke subsequently spent the remainder of his childhood. Worship was an important part of van Dyke's boyhood, both at home and at church. His father was active in various councils of the Presbyterian Church but always found time to take his son on much-loved fishing excursions.

After studies at the Brooklyn Polytechnic Institute, van Dyke enrolled in Princeton University. He was graduated from Princeton with a bachelor of arts degree in 1873 and from Princeton's Theological Seminary in 1877. While at Princeton, van Dyke won honors in English, essays, and oration. Following his graduation, he studied in Berlin and elsewhere throughout Europe for one year; he then returned to the United States to his first pastorate, which was at the United Congregational Church in Newport, Rhode Island. Just before he departed for his new post, van Dyke received the honor of ordination by the Brooklyn Presbytery at his father's own church on Clinton Street.

While serving his church in Rhode Island, van Dyke found himself thinking often of a certain Miss Ellen Reid he had met while still a student at the Princeton Theological Seminary. After learning that Miss Reid was spending the summer on Martha's Vineyard with her sister, van Dyke traveled there often, thus beginning an intense period of courtship. They were married on December 13, 1881; and after nine children and fifty years of happiness, Henry and Ellen van Dyke celebrated their golden wedding anniversary in 1931.

From 1883 to 1899 van Dyke was pastor of the Brick Presbyterian Church in New York, where his sermons became so popular that the congregation often flowed out onto the street. Church attendance increased from 300 to 900 during van Dyke's tenure. *The Story of the Other Wise Man* and *The First Christmas Tree* (originally called *The Oak of Geismar*) were first given as Christmas sermons at the Brick Church and were later translated into at least twenty-eight different languages. In *The Story of the Other Wise Man*, van Dyke describes the journey of Artaban, who attempts to join the wise men in Bethlehem but is waylaid again and again by someone in need. After thirty-three years of trying to reach his Saviour, Artaban dies in the earthquake following the crucifixion. But his dream comes true after all as he sees Christ in heaven. In the foreword to Henry van Dyke's biography, his son Tertius relates that *The Story of the Other Wise Man* came to his father one night "suddenly and without labor." His father wrote it throughout the following months "with meekness and with joy." This inspirational story has touched thousands every year at Christmastime all around the world.

After publishing several books and volumes of poetry, van Dyke gained the respect of the literary world, including great writers such as Mark Twain and James Whitcomb Riley. From 1900 until 1923 he was a member of Princeton University's faculty as the Murray Professor of English Literature, a position from which he resigned on three occasions. He was persuaded to remain after the first two resignations by the heartfelt pleas of the students and fellow faculty members; van Dyke's course was the most popular at Princeton.

In 1912 van Dyke was elected president of the National Institute of Arts and Letters; and the next year he flew overseas to fulfill his newly appointed position as minister to the Netherlands and Luxembourg, a position he accepted from his friend President Woodrow Wilson. With the onset of World War I, van Dyke felt compelled to resign his diplomatic position in a neutral country because his spirit was with the Allied cause. Van Dyke felt so strongly that he volunteered for active service. He served as a lieutenant commander in the Chaplain Corps and received the Cross of the Legion of Honor from France. Van Dyke finally returned to his position at Princeton in 1919, where he remained until he retired in 1923. He died at his home in Princeton, New Jersey, on April 10, 1933.

As a versatile writer of prose and verse as well as a gifted religious leader, Henry van Dyke touched the lives of thousands of Americans. In everything he said or wrote, van Dyke included a deep reverence for God and His creation. This Christmas, as we read *The First Christmas Tree* and *The Story of the Other Wise Man*, whether for the first time or the hundredth, let us remember the story of the writer behind the story, the story of a man who used his talents to serve God all his life.

To An Angel

Dixie Schaefer

You need no wings of wire and net,
No gown of frothy white,
To be a lovely angel in
The Christmas play tonight.

Retarded? Some would say that you're
A child at twenty-three;
But you are so much more than that
To those who really see.

Is it a disability
To spend these years at play,
To dwell on Earth in innocence
Until you fly away?

Your love is unconditional;
It shows in all you do.
So which of us is handicapped?
Am I the one, not you?

Opposite Page
GABRIEL
St. Mary's Church, Michigan City, Indiana
The Crosiers/Gene Plaisted, OSC, Photographer

BITS & PIECES

The best of all gifts around any Christmas tree:
the presence of a happy family all wrapped up
in each other.

Burton Hillis

To cherish peace and goodwill, to be plenteous in mercy,
is to have the real spirit of Christmas. If we think o'er these
things, there will be born in us a Saviour and over us will shine
a star sending its gleam of hope to the world.

Calvin Coolidge

Christmas is the time to let your heart do the thinking.
Patricia Clafford

At Christmas play and make good cheer,
For Christmas comes but once a year.
Thomas Tusser

60

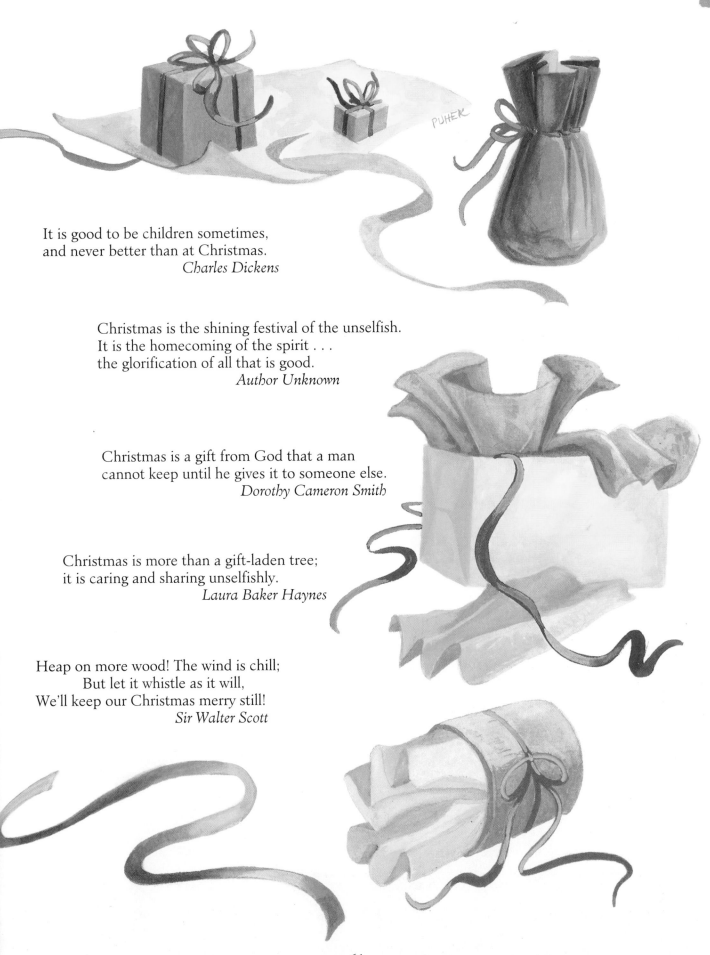

It is good to be children sometimes,
and never better than at Christmas.
Charles Dickens

Christmas is the shining festival of the unselfish.
It is the homecoming of the spirit . . .
the glorification of all that is good.
Author Unknown

Christmas is a gift from God that a man
cannot keep until he gives it to someone else.
Dorothy Cameron Smith

Christmas is more than a gift-laden tree;
it is caring and sharing unselfishly.
Laura Baker Haynes

Heap on more wood! The wind is chill;
But let it whistle as it will,
We'll keep our Christmas merry still!
Sir Walter Scott

Gifts

Elizabeth E. Barnes

For you this Christmastime I wish
So many precious things,
Not only gifts in packages
Secured with tinsel strings
But treasures that are richer far
Than any gold can buy—
A scarlet leaf from Autumn's hills,
A bit of starry sky,
Health and peace, loved ones to share
A hearth fire burning bright,
And in your heart the Song that rang
Across the world that night.

The Christmas She Was Wedded

Loise Pinkerton Fritz

The Christmas snow was falling
As she sat there all alone,
Close by an attic window
In her snow-bound country home.
Beside her stood a weathered trunk;
Its lid was open wide,
And what a sum of treasures
Was hidden there inside.

At once her eyes were focused
On a silver wedding bell;
She heard the organ playing
In the chapel in the dell.

"What God hath joined together,
Let not man put apart . . ."
These words by preacher spoken
Still echoed in her heart.

The Christmas snow was falling
As she touched her wedding ring;
"O, Perfect Love" resounded sweet
While she sat remembering.
Outside the attic window
Puff-white snowflakes softly fell,
Like the Christmas she was wedded
In the chapel in the dell.

Opposite Page: SNOWY SUNDAY. Sugar Hill, New Hampshire. William Johnson, Johnson's Photography.

Ideals'
Family Recipes

Favorite Recipes from the Ideals Family of Readers

Editor's Note: If you'd like us to consider your favorite recipe, please send a typed copy of the recipe along with your name, address, and phone number to Ideals magazine, ATTN: Recipes, P.O. Box 148000, Nashville, Tennessee 37214-8000. We will pay $10 for each recipe used. Recipes cannot be returned.

APRICOT DELIGHT

Empty two 3-ounce packages apricot-flavored gelatin dessert into large bowl. Add two cups boiling water and stir until dissolved. Add two cups cold water and refrigerate until thickened.

Reserving ½ cup juice, drain one 20-ounce can crushed pineapple. In a medium bowl, combine pineapple, 2 sliced bananas, 2 cups miniature marshmallows, and 1 peeled and diced apple. Stir fruit mixture into gelatin. Pour the entire mixture into a 9-x13-x2-inch pan. Chill until firm.

Suggested topping: In a medium saucepan, combine ½ cup pineapple juice, ¾ cup granulated sugar, 1 beaten egg, and 2 tablespoons flour. Over medium heat, bring mixture to a boil and cook for 1 minute, stirring constantly. Remove from heat. Stir in one 8-ounce package cream cheese; cool. In a small bowl, mix one box Dream Whip ac-cording to package directions. Fold into cream cheese mixture. Spread topping over gelatin. Sprinkle ½ cup flaked coconut over all. Serve chilled and store in refrigerator.

Nancy G. Wilson
Kenansville, North Carolina

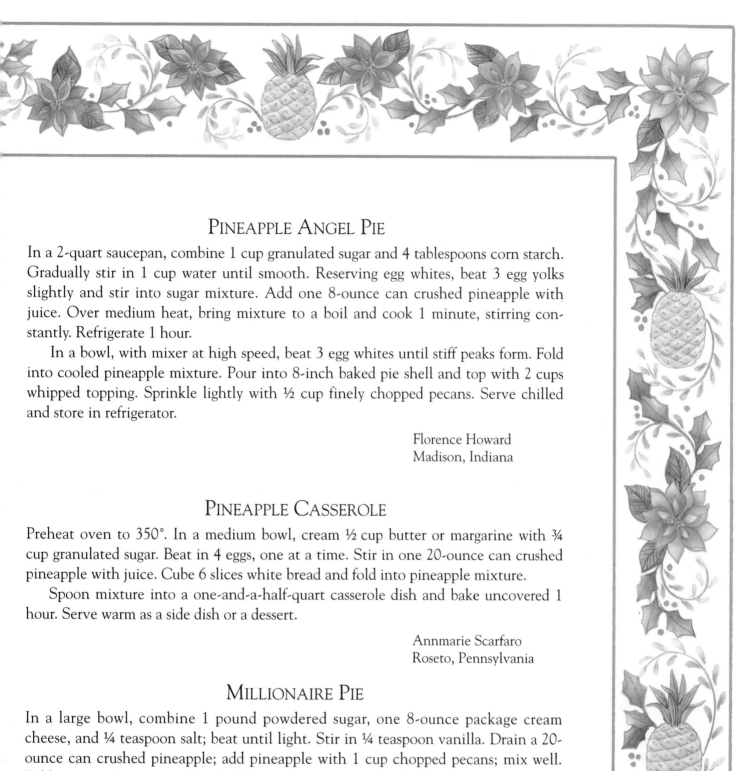

PINEAPPLE ANGEL PIE

In a 2-quart saucepan, combine 1 cup granulated sugar and 4 tablespoons corn starch. Gradually stir in 1 cup water until smooth. Reserving egg whites, beat 3 egg yolks slightly and stir into sugar mixture. Add one 8-ounce can crushed pineapple with juice. Over medium heat, bring mixture to a boil and cook 1 minute, stirring constantly. Refrigerate 1 hour.

In a bowl, with mixer at high speed, beat 3 egg whites until stiff peaks form. Fold into cooled pineapple mixture. Pour into 8-inch baked pie shell and top with 2 cups whipped topping. Sprinkle lightly with ½ cup finely chopped pecans. Serve chilled and store in refrigerator.

Florence Howard
Madison, Indiana

PINEAPPLE CASSEROLE

Preheat oven to 350°. In a medium bowl, cream ½ cup butter or margarine with ¾ cup granulated sugar. Beat in 4 eggs, one at a time. Stir in one 20-ounce can crushed pineapple with juice. Cube 6 slices white bread and fold into pineapple mixture.

Spoon mixture into a one-and-a-half-quart casserole dish and bake uncovered 1 hour. Serve warm as a side dish or a dessert.

Annmarie Scarfaro
Roseto, Pennsylvania

MILLIONAIRE PIE

In a large bowl, combine 1 pound powdered sugar, one 8-ounce package cream cheese, and ¼ teaspoon salt; beat until light. Stir in ¼ teaspoon vanilla. Drain a 20-ounce can crushed pineapple; add pineapple with 1 cup chopped pecans; mix well. Fold in one 16-ounce carton whipped topping. Pour into two 8-inch pie shells. Serve chilled.

Kathleen Boehm
Kansas City, Missouri

The Christmas Holly

Eliza Cook

The holly! The holly! Oh, twine it with bay!
    Come give the holly a song,
For it helps to drive stern winter away,
    With his garment so somber and long.

It peeps through the trees with its berries of red
    And its leaves of burnished green
When the flowers and fruits have long been dead
    And not even the daisy is seen.

Then sing to the holly, the Christmas holly,
    That hangs over peasant and king!
While we laugh and carouse
       'neath its glittering boughs,
    To the Christmas holly we'll sing.

The gale may whistle; the frost may come
    To fetter the gurgling rill;
The woods may be bare, and warblers dumb,
    But holly is beautiful still.

In the revel and light of princely halls
    The bright holly branch is found;
And its shadow falls on the lowliest walls
    While the brimming horn goes round.

The ivy lives long, but its home must be
    Where graves and ruins are spread;
There's beauty about the cypress tree,
    But it flourishes near the dead;

The laurel the warrior's brow may wreathe,
    But it tells of tears and blood;
I sing the holly, and who can breathe
    Aught of that that is not good?

Then sing to the holly, the Christmas holly,
    That hangs over peasant and king;
While we laugh and carouse
       'neath its glittering boughs,
    To the Christmas holly we'll sing.

From My Garden Journal

by Deana Deck

TOPIARY

Until recently, whenever I heard the word "topiary," I pictured vast country estates adorned with decorative animals formed from carefully pruned boxwoods, yews, or hollies. Once I saw a picture of what has to be the ultimate topiary: a fox hunt complete with hounds, horses, and, of course, a running, leafy green fox. The idea of using topiary indoors seemed inconceivable to me.

Well, things have changed, and topiary is now a viable decorating option indoors as well as outside in the garden. Topiary is especially popular for holiday decorating, which is exciting news for anyone who enjoys crafts and yearns for something different to grace their mantel or dining room table this year. Even better news is that topiary does not have to be difficult at all; it doesn't even have to be alive.

There are three types of topiaries. The first is the living plant in a container sculpted meticulously throughout the year and moved indoors to be decorated for the holidays. A topiary of this type usually takes the standard form: a tall trunk supporting a perfectly shaped blooming ball. A topiary standard can be created from poinsettias, fuschias, chrysanthemums, and other flowering, potted plants. Some of the most spectacular examples of this living form of topiary are presented annually at the Chrysanthemum festival at Longwood Gardens in Kennet Square, Pennsylvania. Expert gardeners there train mums into huge hanging ball forms as well as columns, collars, and other shapes. They go way beyond the standard in their topiary designs. They have even created a blooming table complete with two blooming chairs!

The second type of topiary is the "stuffed and planted" variety. This technique can be used to create animal forms, balls, cylinders, or wreaths. A wire form filled with moist sphagnum moss or Oasis® foam is the basis. The form is disguised with moss held in place with thin florist's wire. Cuttings from easily rooted plants such as

TOPIARY

ivy, herbs, wintercreeper euonymus, or Wandering Jew are dipped in rooting hormone and inserted into previously prepared holes poked into the planting medium. The medium is kept moist in a 75° environment. Once the plants have taken root, the piece can be decorated with ribbons, Christmas balls, or artificial fruits and nuts. Some of the most spectacular stuffed and planted forms allow you to create living miniature cone-shaped Christmas trees, wreaths, and bells. Custom-built forms can also be used to make Santas, angels, or even reindeer.

The third and easiest topiary for the inexperienced gardener to create at home is the dried topiary. Dried flowers and fruits as well as styrofoam blocks and preshaped forms are available in local craft or art supply stores. A three-tiered topiary tree is easily constructed by attaching three styrofoam balls to a dowel rod "stem" inserted in a foam-packed, terracotta container. (Clay pots are ideal because their weight tends to help balance the weight of a tall topiary arrangement.) The balls and stem can then be decorated using dried plant material collected from your own garden or purchased from the florist. Artificial flowers and greenery can also be used. The crafter's best friends in a project of this kind are thin, green florist's wire and a hot-glue gun.

If you'd like to include a topiary in your holiday decorating this year but don't feel you have the time to make your own, talk

I found the materials I needed for my topiary project at the craft store down the street. I was even able to use clippings from my own garden!

with your local florist or an interior decorator. Both usually have access to suppliers.

Several good books on the market can inspire and inform you if you want to pursue making your own topiaries, either in the garden or indoors. One is the informative *The New Topiary—Imaginative Techniques from Longwood Gardens*. It includes photos and diagrams of many of the forms displayed at Longwood and has excellent plant listings and sources for obtaining topiary forms and materials.

Another good book is called *Decorating with Wreaths, Garlands and Topiaries*. It also includes photography and step-by-step instructions arranged in seasonal order, which means it offers decorating ideas beyond Christmas. Sources and a reading list are also included.

If you're feeling a bit adventurous this holiday season and want to try your hand at topiary, pick the form and method right for you and have fun!

Deana Deck lives in Nashville, Tennessee, where her garden column is a regular feature in The Tennessean.

Handmade Heirloom

Mary Skarmeas

CHRISTMAS CANDLES. Jessie Walker Associates.

THE ART OF CANDLEMAKING

The soft glow of candlelight is a familiar and treasured part of our lives: elegant silver candelabras add to the grandeur of a formal dinner; heirloom candlesticks—found in grandma's attic or stored in an antique hutch—give family celebrations a deeper sense of tradition; a single, flickering candle casts a magic spell over a cozy supper for two; and candles lit in reverence shine in our places of worship, adding grace and beauty to our religious ceremonies. Despite the easy availability of more efficient lighting options, candlelight maintains its hold on our imaginations.

Although the exact origin of the candle is unknown, a bronze candleholder found in the tomb of Tutankhamen is evidence that candles have been used at least since the days of the Egyptian pharaohs. The word "candle" comes from the Latin *candere* meaning "to shine"; this leads us to believe that candles were also part of early Roman culture. Iron and clay candleholders have been found at ancient sites in Greece, China, and Japan. The earliest actual candle remnant was discovered in France and has been dated to the first century A.D.

In all cultures, candles have served a dual

function: practical everyday lighting and the symbolic lighting of religious and ceremonial observances. At baptisms, weddings, and funerals, candles serve as symbols of divine guidance, of vows made and kept, of hope for the future, and of remembrance of the past. Placing candles in the window is an old German custom meant to welcome passing angels. Similarly, in America today we also light our windows with candles—electric, of course!—at Christmastime as a symbol of welcome to weary travelers. Through the years, the line between practical and symbolic use has blurred; but no matter what our religion or tradition, we are all thankful for candles when natural disasters leave us without electricity!

The appeal—and necessity—of candles in modern life is most evident in the constant popularity of the craft of candlemaking. In the United States alone well over 40 million pounds of paraffin are used for candlemaking each year. With a little knowledge of proper techniques, materials, and supplies, anyone can create lovely and useful candles in styles that recreate the traditional taper candle or in any number of shapes, colors, scents, and designs.

Early candles were made from tallow (rendered animal fat), which burned poorly and had an unpleasant odor, or from beeswax, which burned evenly and smelled sweetly of honey but was more difficult to get because the churches and temples used most of what was available. Bees were thought to be closely associated with the spirit world, and their wax was considered essential by many churches for candles intended for religious purposes.

Although the bee is not held in such high esteem today, beeswax is still very popular for making candles. They are the simplest candles to make, although the wax remains very expensive. Beeswax comes in rectangular sheets stripped from the honeycomb. The sheets are cut into triangles for candlemaking and can be purchased ready to roll. A length of candlewicking is placed at the long end and the slightly warmed wax is gently rolled around it. The bottom is sealed by tamping in a warm pan. Beeswax candles are lightweight, slow-burning, and delicately scented.

The oldest method of candlemaking is dipping. A wick, usually made of flax or cotton fiber, is carefully dipped into melted wax or fat and removed to cool and solidify in the air. Successive dippings build up the candle to its desired thickness. Dipping is time consuming but still done today, although few candlemakers make use of tallow. Most candle wax used today is a store-bought mixture of paraffin wax and stearic acid.

A wonderful exception is the bayberry candle, made from the wax of the berries picked from the bay bush, a small shrub found along the eastern coast of North America. Bayberries are small dark berries covered with greenish-white wax. Early settlers of Cape Cod, Massachusetts, used the plentiful bayberries they found around their homes to make distinctly aromatic candles. The custom continues today, and the scent of the bayberry is a familiar one at Christmastime in many American homes. In making bayberry candles, small batches of berries are boiled for five minutes and left to cool until the wax rises to the top. The wax is then skimmed off the top and the process repeated until all berries have been used. The wax is remelted and strained to get rid of all impurities and then stored in tightly sealed containers. It can be formed into candles by dipping, as described above, or by molding. All of the traditional methods of candlemaking are easily imitated today—look in your local library or craft store for more detailed instructions.

The simple beeswax candle and the bayberry candle are lovely examples of a decorative and useful craft that will bring many hours of enjoyment and satisfaction. And while candles are not, strictly speaking, heirlooms, they appeal to the same need that inspires collectors of antique handmade quilts or dolls—their presence in our homes links us to the past and is a symbol of the importance of tradition in our lives. The invention of electric light has not made the candle obsolete; on the contrary, the charm of the soft glow of candlelight is treasured all the more by those of us who live with the modern alternative.

Mary Skarmeas lives in Danvers, Massachusetts, and is studying for her bachelor's degree in English at Suffolk University. Mother of four and grandmother of one, Mary loves all crafts, especially knitting.

Living Candles

Reginald Holmes

If you left the Christmas spirit
  Tucked away upon the shelf,
Take it down and start the season
  By the giving of yourself.

Just by saying, "Merry Christmas"
  With a smile upon your face,
You can make some person happy
  And the world a better place.

If life's hardly worth the living,
  Find yourself a worthy cause:
Take that basket to the needy;
  Make believe you're Santa Claus.

If the spark of faith is feeble,
  You may well be reconciled
If you read the Christmas story
  To a lonely little child.

If you're someone who is looking
  For a mission to fulfill,
Be a living Christmas candle
  On the world's wide windowsill.

"GOODNIGHT, CANDLELIGHT"
D. Petku/H. Armstrong Roberts

Christmas Reflections

Iris W. Bray

Scenes of Christmas swiftly change,
Then fade, like melting snow.
The season's joys too soon become
A hazy afterglow.

The festive lights are vanished;
Once splendid trees are bare;
Sacred chimes and carols
No longer fill the air.

Ornaments and keepsakes,
The wreath upon the door,
The tinsel and the trimmings
Are set aside to store.

All symbols of the season
Are packed and shelved to stay,
But the miracle that is Christmas
Cannot be tucked away!

The royal star, the angel song,
The Christ Child's holy birth—
All peace and hope and gladness
Like a mantle round the earth.

The symbols but remind us
Of the season we hold dear,
But if Christ be born within us,
Christmas stays forever near!

SAWTOOTH NATIONAL RECREATION AREA
Salmon River, Idaho
Superstock Photo

Readers' Forum

Meet Our *Ideals* Readers and Their Families

IRMA FORD of Drumheller, Alberta, in Canada sent us this photograph of her granddaughter Michelle Scobie, who is whispering her dreams to Santa Claus. Michelle lives in Grande Prairie, Alberta, with her sister Colette and her parents Brenda and Norman. Since Grande Prairie is about eight hours away from Drumheller, Irma doesn't see her daughter and her family often, but they all usually visit at Christmas each year. In addition to Michelle and Colette, Irma has three more grandchildren.

Irma loves to share her *Ideals* subscription with everyone at the Seniors' Lodge where she is Activities Coordinator. When she's not busy there, she likes to crochet baby blankets and pot holders and read *Ideals*.

MARIA WOODSON in Raleigh, North Carolina, wanted to share with the *Ideals* family this picture of her parents' living room decorated for the holiday season. Since this is the home where Maria grew up, it is especially meaningful to her to be able to take her five-year-old son Michael there each year for Christmas.

Maria grew up reading her mother's copies of *Ideals* and finally got her own subscription. When she's not reading *Ideals'* poetry to Michael, Maria is studying to become an elementary school teacher. She often practices what she studies on Michael to see the immediate results!

This is Elaina Rae Romero struggling to hold on to her pooch Misty and pose for a Christmas portrait at the same time. HELEN CYPHERS in Camino, California, sent us this photo of her great-granddaughter who lives with her mother, Melinda, in Lincoln, California.

Helen calls Camino, California, a lovely little hamlet hidden up in the mountains. When she isn't visiting with her four grandchildren or two great-grandchildren, Helen loves to work in her garden, where she grows tulips, petunias, and beautiful red roses.

Thank you Irma Ford, Maria Woodson, and Helen Cyphers for sharing with *Ideals* this Christmas. We hope to hear from other readers who would like to share photos and stories with the *Ideals* family. Please include a self-addressed, stamped envelope if you would like the photos returned. Keep your original photographs for safekeeping and send duplicate photos along with your name, address, and telephone number to:

Readers' Forum
Ideals Publications Inc.
P.O. Box 148000
Nashville, TN 37214-8000

Publisher, Patricia A. Pingry
Editor, Lisa C. Thompson
Art Director, Patrick McRae
Copy Editor, Laura Matter
Editorial Assistant, Crystal Edison
Contributing Editors, Lansing Christman, Deana Deck, Russ Flint, Pamela Kennedy, Mary Skarmeas, Nancy Skarmeas

ACKNOWLEDGMENTS

PA DID IT from *RHYMES OF CHILDHOOD* by Edgar Guest, copyright ©1924 by the Reilly & Lee Co., used by permission of the author's estate. Our sincere thanks to the following authors whom we were unable to contact: Elizabeth E. Barnes for GIFTS; Reginald Holmes for LIVING CANDLES; and Blanche Elizabeth Wade for THE SONG OF THE CHRISTMAS TREE.

ANNOUNCING A BEAUTIFUL NEW WAY TO GREET EACH DAY
THE *ideals* 1995 PERSONAL CALENDAR

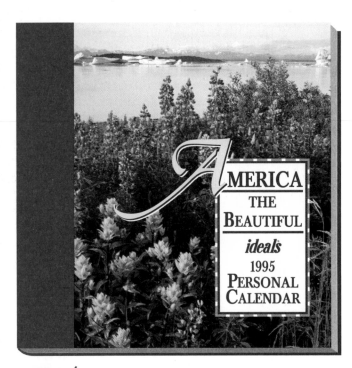

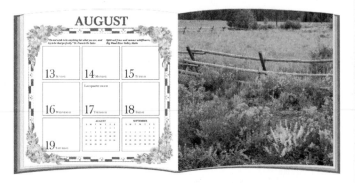

This exquisitely beautiful Personal Calendar has been designed and produced especially for the *Ideals* reader who appreciates the spectacular grandeur of the natural world and the touching sentiments of people such as Ralph Waldo Emerson, Elizabeth Barrett Browning, and Henry Wadsworth Longfellow.

BREATHTAKING PHOTOS OF MAGNIFICENT BEAUTY

Every week you'll step into a different setting, each more breathtaking than the one before. Over 50 magnificent full-color photographs from award-winning photographer Jeff Gnass take you to places like

Yosemite Falls on a sunny morning, Bass Harbor Head Lighthouse at sunset, the Grand Tetons at sunrise, the Monterey Peninsula overlooking the Pacific Ocean, and more, each selected by photographer Gnass for its beauty and creative artistry.

HEARTFELT WORDS OF INSPIRATION

Each week begins with a line or two of inspiring words that capture the beauty and uniqueness of each week of the year. In addition, each photograph is identified as to its location in our majestic country.

AMPLE ROOM FOR WRITING

There's plenty of space to write notes each day of the year, and the miniature calendars for the current month and the upcoming month make planning your whole year a breeze while the attractive and whimsical artistic borders brighten each week.

SCENIC COVER WITH QUALITY CLOTH SPINE

This lovely hardbound calendar features a lay-flat, stitched binding, matte paper, and quality cloth spine, all of which make an attractive book to keep on your shelf as a reminder of the year.